Learning Musical Instruments

Should I Play the
Guitar?

Richard Spilsbury

Heinemann Library
Chicago, Illinois

Customer Service 888-454-2279
Visit our website at www.heinemannraintree.com

Designed by Richard Parker and Manhattan Design
Illustrations by Jeff Edwards
Printed and bound in China by Leo Paper Group

11 10 09 08 07
10 9 8 7 6 5 4 3 2 1

Library of Congress Cataloging-in-Publication Data
Spilsbury, Richard, 1963-
  Should I play the guitar? / Richard Spilsbury.
     p. cm. -- (Learning musical instruments)
  Includes bibliographical references (p.   ), discography, and index.
  ISBN 1-4034-8188-1 (library binding - hardcover)
 1. Guitar Juvenile literature. I. Title. II. Series.
  ML1015.G9S66 2006
  787.87--dc22   2006006673

Acknowledgments
The publishers would like to thank the following for permission to reproduced photographs:
Alamy p. **27** (David Young-Wolff); Bridgeman Art Library p. **7** (The Iveagh Bequest, Kenwood House,
London, UK The Guitar Player, c. 1672 (oil on canvas), Vermeer, Jan (1632–75)); Corbis pp. **4** (Philip
Gould), **6** (Zefa/Anna Peisl), **12** (Rune Hellestad), **15** (Lynn Goldsmith); Getty Images pp. **9** (Photodisc),
17, **21**; Harcourt Education Ltd/Tudor Photography pp. **5**, **13**, **24**, **24**, **25**, **26**; Lebrecht pp. **8**
(Photographers Direct), **14** (Richard Haughton); Photoedit p.**19** (Bob Daemmrich); Redferns pp. **18**
(Nicky J. Sims), **20** (Peter Still), **22** (Stephan Engler); Richard Parker p. **10**; Topfoto pp. **16**, **23**.

Cover image of the Edge playing the guitar reproduced with permission of Retna.

The publishers would like to thank Teryl Dobbs for her assistance in the preparation of this book.

Contents

Any words appearing in the text in bold, **like this**, are explained in the Glossary.

Why Do People Play Musical Instruments?

People around the world play musical instruments for lots of reasons. A few people play or teach guitar as a job. They have spent many, many hours practicing and playing in order to become very good. However, most people play and practice their guitar just because they like it. They also get a thrill from making music for their own and other people's pleasure.

Guitars are easy to play and carry around, which allows you to share your music with others.

FROM THE EXPERTS

"Music is the art of thinking with sounds."

Jules Combarieu, writer on music

"The guitar is your first wings. It's ... designed to unfold your vision and imagination."

Carlos Santana, famous rock guitarist

Music and emotions

Music is something that lots of people understand, even when they do not have a spoken language in common. When we play or listen to music, we may feel happy, thoughtful, or sad. We can even forget what we are actually doing and imagine different worlds, or we may think about important things in our lives.

Music is a great reason to meet up. We can share the experience of music-making in bands, school **orchestras** and groups, in the classroom, or with friends at home. We can share the excitement of hearing great music on the concert stage.

Learning to play an instrument properly takes time, but is well worth the effort.

Music and learning

Many people believe that playing an instrument helps you learn other things. For example, you learn about history when you look at the lives of **composers**, and you learn about math when you count beats in music. The main thing you learn, though, is that playing music is lots of fun!

What Is a Guitar?

A guitar is a **string instrument**. You play it by **plucking** single strings or **strumming** lots of strings in **chords**. Guitarists either sit or stand while playing the strings with one hand and pressing strings down to change notes with the other.

You can practice your guitar almost anywhere! It is best to find a quiet place where you will not be disturbed or distracted.

History of guitars

Different string instruments have been around for many hundreds of years. One of the first that looked a bit like today's guitars was the vihuela (pronounced "vee-hoo-ay-la") from the 1400s in Spain. It had twelve strings, several holes in the front, and **frets** to show players where to put their fingers on the strings to get different notes. Its strings were arranged in six **courses**, which means six sets of doubled strings.

Guitars developed from the vihuela in Spain in the 1500s. These guitars were smaller than today's guitars. They were easier to play than vihuelas because they had four or five courses and wider **fingerboards**. In the 1850s a Spanish guitar-maker named Antonio de Torres Jurado started to make better guitars. They were large and made of thin, light wood, but they were still strong. They had six single strings that were close to the fingerboard and a big hole in the center. All these changes meant it was easier to play different notes on a Torres guitar, with a richer, louder sound.

The woman in this 1672 painting by Jan Vermeer is playing an early guitar.

Most guitar bodies today are still made of wood, but some are made partly of plastic or even metal.

GUITAR FACTS: Different shapes

Today, many guitars are very similar to the "Torres pattern." However, there are different shapes for different music. For example, arch-top guitars were developed to play loud **jazz**. They have a curved wooden top, f-shaped holes similar to those in a violin, and tight steel strings to make a loud sound.

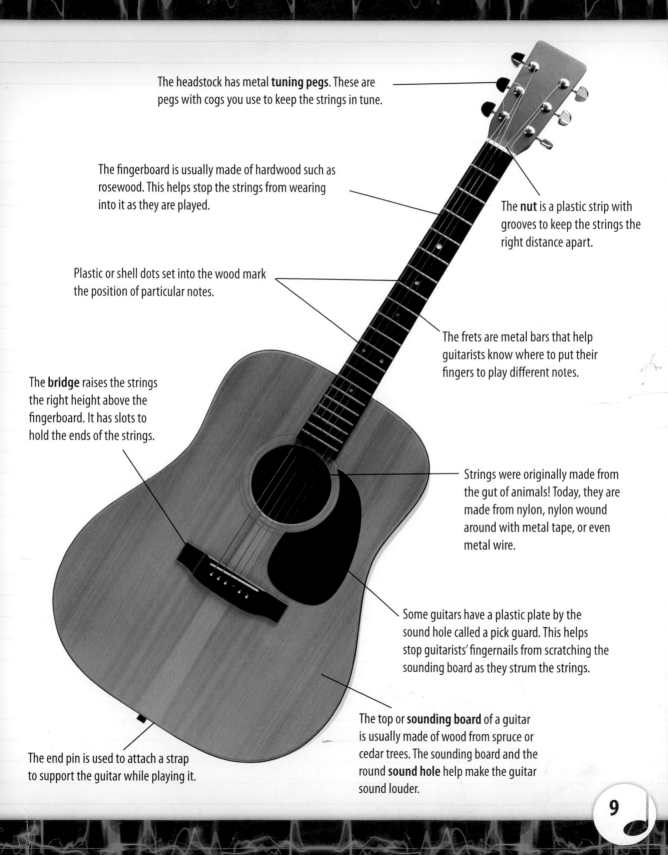

The headstock has metal **tuning pegs**. These are pegs with cogs you use to keep the strings in tune.

The fingerboard is usually made of hardwood such as rosewood. This helps stop the strings from wearing into it as they are played.

The **nut** is a plastic strip with grooves to keep the strings the right distance apart.

Plastic or shell dots set into the wood mark the position of particular notes.

The frets are metal bars that help guitarists know where to put their fingers to play different notes.

The **bridge** raises the strings the right height above the fingerboard. It has slots to hold the ends of the strings.

Strings were originally made from the gut of animals! Today, they are made from nylon, nylon wound around with metal tape, or even metal wire.

Some guitars have a plastic plate by the sound hole called a pick guard. This helps stop guitarists' fingernails from scratching the sounding board as they strum the strings.

The top or **sounding board** of a guitar is usually made of wood from spruce or cedar trees. The sounding board and the round **sound hole** help make the guitar sound louder.

The end pin is used to attach a strap to support the guitar while playing it.

9

How Does a Guitar Make Its Sound?

If you stretch a rubber band between the two ends of a ruler and **pluck** it, the band makes a "twang" sound. Things that **vibrate** back and forth, such as plucked rubber bands or guitar strings, push aside invisible ripples of air. It is similar to the waves in a pond after you drop a stone in the water. We call the ripples **sound waves** because our ears hear them as sounds.

This photo shows how a stretched guitar string bends as it vibrates.

Different pitches

Each guitar string plays a different note, or **pitch**, depending on how tight, heavy, or long it is. Tight strings create higher pitches than loose strings because they vibrate faster. We make sure the pitch of each string is right before playing a guitar by tuning it. This is done by turning the **tuning pegs** to tighten or loosen each string.

Strings also vibrate faster when they are light, because there is less weight to move through the air. That is why the lowest-pitch strings on guitars are made of thicker, heavier material than higher-pitch strings.

Guitar strings normally vibrate between the **nut** and the **bridge**. We change notes on a guitar string by pressing it with a finger against a **fret**. Then, the only bit of string that vibrates is between that fret and the bridge. This section of string is now shorter, so it makes a higher pitch.

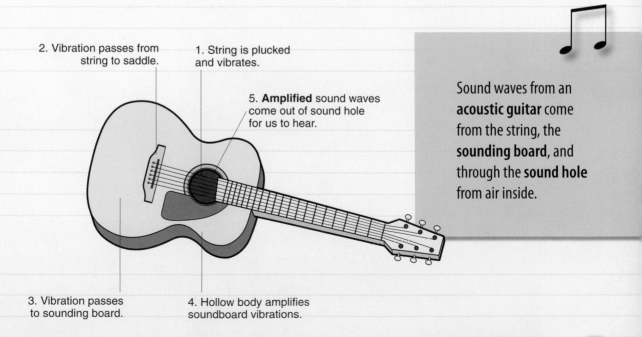

2. Vibration passes from string to saddle.

1. String is plucked and vibrates.

5. **Amplified** sound waves come out of sound hole for us to hear.

3. Vibration passes to sounding board.

4. Hollow body amplifies soundboard vibrations.

Sound waves from an **acoustic guitar** come from the string, the **sounding board**, and through the **sound hole** from air inside.

Electric guitar sound

Electric guitars usually have very thin metal strings. Instead of a sounding board, they have pickups underneath the strings. Pickups are special magnets that turn a string's vibration into an electrical signal. These signals travel along a cable from the guitar to an electric machine called an **amplifier**. The amplifier makes the signals bigger and changes them into big sound waves.

Electric guitars amplify their sound without a sounding board or hollow body.

GUITAR FACTS: The log

Les Paul built the first electric guitar with a solid (not hollow) body in 1941. He put a **fingerboard**, strings, and pickups onto a thick block of wood. He called it "the log." People liked the sound of the log, but not how it looked. So, Les cut a hollow **jazz** guitar into two and glued the halves onto it!

Holding the guitar

Many people sit down to play guitar. They can then support the body of the instrument comfortably on the right thigh. Other guitarists stand to play, supporting the instrument using a strap that goes from the headstock to the end pin (see page 9).

The left-hand thumb then rests on the back of the guitar neck, while the fingers curl around to the front. Then, the fingertips can press the strings toward the neck to change notes. The right hand should **strum** the strings, moving from the wrist rather than the elbow. Some left-handed players reverse this and strum with their left hand.

Make sure that you are relaxed and comfortable when you practice your guitar.

Changing the sound

Guitarists can change the sound they make in different ways. For example, any note or **chord** sounds softer if you play it using fingertips than it does when played with hard fingernails or a plastic pick. The type of strings also changes the sound. Metal strings make a brighter, harsher sound than nylon strings.

Which Musical Family Are Guitars From?

String instruments are one of five families of musical instruments. Some string instruments, such as violins and cellos, are played with a bow. A bow has tight hairs on it that are rubbed across the strings. This can make the strings **vibrate** longer than if they are **plucked**. Guitars are plucked or **strummed**.

Other types of plucked instruments

There are lots of different instruments that are plucked, apart from guitars. These include banjos and harps. Banjos have a round drum skin tightly stretched around metal to **amplify** their sound. Harps have a wooden or metal frame with lots of different length strings stretched across it. Both hands are used to pluck or strum patterns of strings to play different **pitches**.

The largest string instrument played with a bow is the double bass.

Different guitars

Different types of guitar produce different sounds. For example, some **acoustic guitars** have very big bodies and six **courses** of strings to make a bigger, richer sound than normal. The bass guitar and Mexican Tres have just the lowest four strings of a normal six-string guitar. The guitarist plays patterns of low notes to **accompany** tunes with higher notes played on other instruments. Some bass guitars have an extra lower string to play very deep notes.

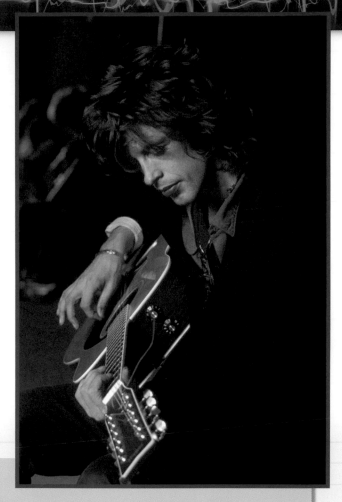

Each course on a twelve-string guitar has two close strings. The four lowest notes have a second string that is an **octave** higher and the two highest notes have a second string that is the same.

GUITAR FACTS: Jumping flea

Ukuleles are Hawaiian plucked instruments that are like tiny guitars, but with four strings. They were first brought to Hawaii by Portuguese settlers. There is a story that the name comes from the Hawaiian word for "jumping flea." This is because a very good Portuguese player was changing notes so quickly that his fingers were dancing around like fleas!

Plucked instruments from around the world

The *gopichand* from eastern India has just one string stretched tightly by two curved pieces of bamboo. A *gopichand* player plucks the string and bends the bamboo together. This stretches or loosens the string so that it plays sliding notes.

The *sitar* is from northern India. It generally has a hollowed-out pumpkin for a body and a long, hollow wooden neck. *Sitar* players change notes on the four main strings by pressing strings against curved metal **frets**. There are another eleven strings of different lengths that vibrate beneath the frets.

The *kora* is from West Africa. It is like a rounded drum, with a round, wooden stick neck. Twenty-one strings of different lengths run from different points on the neck over a notched **bridge** resting on the drum skin.

Kora players rest both hands on hand posts to pluck the strings with thumb and forefinger.

What Types of Music Can You Play on a Guitar?

One of the great things about the guitar is that it can be used to play most styles of music—from **strummed folk** songs and elegant **classical** tunes to the fast **solos** of **blues** and **rock**. The possibilities are endless!

Folk music

Folk is the traditional, popular songs that are shared and known within a community. The first guitars were cheap, simple instruments widely played by and for **peasants** in Europe.

Many places around the world have their own styles of folk music, from Mexican mariachi to Spanish flamenco (see page 22). Many of these include the guitar sound. There are also mixtures of different styles of folk music. One example in the United States is **country and western** music.

Jack Johnson plays a mixture of folk, blues, and rock on his **acoustic guitar**.

Classical music

In the 1600s people did not write classical music to be performed on the guitar. This was partly because the guitar was thought to be a peasant instrument. It was also because the guitar was too quiet to be heard in **orchestras**. In the 1800s some guitarists adapted music by classical **composers** such as Johann Sebastian Bach for the new, improved Torres guitar. Others, such as Fernando Sor, wrote pieces especially for guitar. In 1940 Joaquín Rodrigo wrote the *Concierto de Aranjuez* for guitar and orchestra. It is still one of the most frequently played of all guitar **concertos** today.

John Williams is a highly respected classical guitarist.

There is lots of great classical music to play on the acoustic guitar. In some schools there are guitar groups, so lots of guitarists can play classical music together. This is a great way to see and hear how others play and to make a big guitar sound together.

Blues and jazz

Both acoustic and **electric guitars** are important instruments in blues and **jazz** music. Blues and jazz are partly written down and partly made up, or **improvised**. That means guitarists can play tunes in a very personal way. The first blues recordings were made in the early 1900s, but the music had been around much longer. It was developed by African-American musicians in the southern United States. They were influenced by many things, including the music of African slaves who had lived there. Blues led to the development of jazz, which often has a more irregular rhythm.

If you are the kind of musician who likes to create your own music, maybe you should give blues or jazz a try. You do not have to be able to improvise much at first.

There is lots of music to help you learn and there are lots of groups, such as school bands, to take part in.

Rock music

Rock is loud, exciting music, usually played on electric guitar. Rock started in the 1950s when musicians such as Chuck Berry mixed up bits of blues music and folk music to make a style that lots of people enjoyed. The electric guitar solo of fast, **plucked** notes is very important in styles of rock such as heavy metal. Playing fast rhythms of guitar **chords** is more important in styles such as punk. The best ways to learn rock guitar are by playing along to favorite CDs and by forming or joining a school rock group.

FROM THE EXPERTS

"I'd play whenever I could get my hands on an electric guitar; I was trying to pick up ... electric blues—the latest Muddy Waters. I'd spend hours and hours on the same track, back again and back again."

Keith Richards, guitarist in The Rolling Stones

The power of electric guitars is one reason bands like Green Day are so exciting to listen to.

Who Plays the Guitar?

About 50 million people play the guitar worldwide, but only a few become famous guitarists. These guitarists all have the ability to play the instrument amazingly well. They also make people feel emotions when listening to their music.

Classical guitarists

One of the most important **classical** guitarists was Andrés Segovia (1893–1987), who was from Linares, in Spain. He was taught violin and piano when young, but fell in love with the guitar. His parents, friends, and teachers thought this instrument was not right for classical music. Andrés was so convinced the guitar should be played in concert halls, just like the violin, that he taught himself. He did this so well that by the age of sixteen he gave his first public concerts.

Andrés's concerts and recordings encouraged more people to play and compose for classical guitar. He also taught other famous guitarists, such as Julian Bream. Many of today's top classical guitarists learned using Andrés's methods. Some well-known names include Christopher Parkening, Ricardo Cobo, Lily Afshar, and the Romero family.

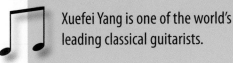

Xuefei Yang is one of the world's leading classical guitarists.

GUITAR FACTS: Flamenco

Flamenco is a style of **folk** music from southern Spain. Flamenco guitarists play wild, powerful music with fast, complicated rhythms to accompany singers and dancers. The best can rapidly improvise solos like the best jazz players.

Jazz guitarists

One of the biggest names in **jazz** was Belgian guitarist Django Reinhardt (1910–1953). Django could not read music and taught himself how to **improvise** on the **acoustic guitar**. Django's left hand was so badly burned when he was eighteen that he could only use two fingers to change notes. This did not stop him from becoming famous for his fantastic, fast, and fun guitar playing.

Charlie Christian lived around the same time as Django, but in the U.S. He was the first great jazz musician to use the **electric guitar**. Today's top jazz electric guitarists include John McLaughlin, Pat Metheny, and John Scofield.

Paco de Lucía is one of the greatest flamenco guitarists.

Blues and rock guitarists

Muddy Waters (1915–1983), from Mississippi, was one of the most famous **blues** guitarists of all time. Before Muddy, few blues guitarists played electric guitar. Muddy played powerfully and with great feeling to **accompany** his own singing. His popular electric blues sound influenced other great blues players, such as B. B. King. It also influenced some of the most famous **rock** guitarists ever, such as Eric Clapton and Jimi Hendrix. Jimi Hendrix (1942–1970) could play rhythm **chords** while also playing a fast **solo** at the same time. He used his **amplifier** to create new electric guitar sounds. Jimi's sound influenced many famous rock guitarists, including Stevie Ray Vaughan and Tom Morello.

Jimi Hendrix was a left-handed guitarist, but he played a right-handed guitar upside down! It was specially restrung so the low strings were still at the top.

FROM THE EXPERTS

"The guitar is a small **orchestra**. Every string is a different color, a different voice."

Andrés Segovia

How Would I Learn to Play the Guitar?

Before you buy a guitar, borrow or rent one first to see if it is the right instrument for you. Once you know it is, you can choose from many guitars at different price levels at good music stores.

Choosing your instrument

Play a few guitars to find one that is the right size and has a sound you like. Here are some things to look out for:

- Look down the **fingerboard** to see that it is flat and that all the **frets** stick out the same amount. This will make notes easier to play.
- Turn the **tuning pegs** to check that they move easily but are stiff enough to stop the strings from getting loose. Otherwise it will be difficult to keep your guitar in tune.

There are lots of different styles of guitar to choose from, including colorful electric ones!

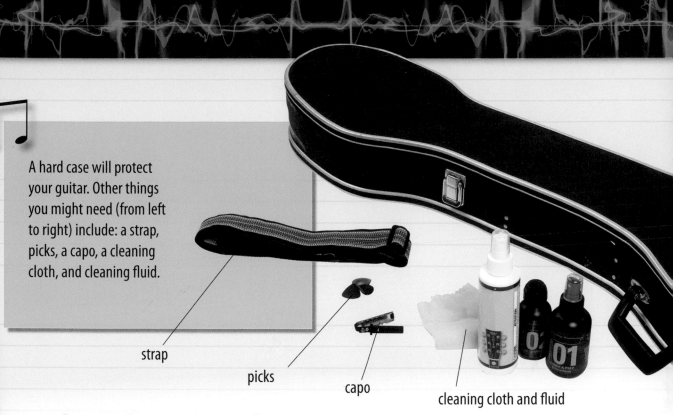

A hard case will protect your guitar. Other things you might need (from left to right) include: a strap, picks, a capo, a cleaning cloth, and cleaning fluid.

strap

picks

capo

cleaning cloth and fluid

Acoustic or electric?

Many people recommend an **acoustic guitar** to learn on. They are usually cheaper than **electric guitars**, and you will not need to buy an **amplifier**. Electric guitar strings are always thin metal and can make your fingertips sore when you play them. However, the strings are closer together and easier for people with small hands to play than full-size acoustic guitars. Your choice depends partly on the style of music you want to play.

What else will I need?

- A pick to **pluck** the strings
- A case to protect your guitar when you are not using it
- A strap to support the guitar if you play standing up
- A tuning aid. This can be electronic or something you blow into to get different **pitches**. You tune the guitar strings to match these pitches.
- A soft cloth to wipe grease from your hands off the strings and fingerboard.

Getting started

Some of the greatest guitarists could not read music and learned to play by copying and watching others. Some people still do this. However, most people think it is best to learn guitar by reading music. It is easiest to do this with a teacher. Teachers can show you where to place your fingers to play different notes and **chords**. They will show you how to **strum** and pluck to get the best sound, as well as many other things. A recommendation from another guitarist is a good way to find a guitar teacher. However, your school, local music store, or library may also be able to help in your search.

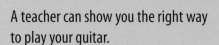

A teacher can show you the right way to play your guitar.

GUITAR FACTS: Tabs

Tablatures, or tabs, are diagrams of the guitar strings. They show frets and the finger positions needed to play different chords. Tabs can be used without reading music. Printed music of pop songs often shows tabs to go with the singing part.

Getting better

It is very important to practice if you want to become a better guitarist. Set yourself targets of learning a few notes or chords each week. Learn pieces of music bit by bit before trying to play the whole thing. Practice slowly before building up your speed.

Try to join a group. It really helps you to keep in tune, in time, and to fit in with the sounds of other musicians. Listen to great guitarists on CDs and the radio. You can also watch them on TV or at concerts. They will help you understand more about the possibilities of your instrument.

Always practice in a quiet place and make time to practice a little each day.

Recordings to Listen To

Classical

Julian Bream, *Spanish Guitar Recital* (RCA Classical Navigator, 2004)

Andrés Segovia, *Andrés Segovia: The Centenary Celebration* (MCA, 1994)

There are lots of versions of Rodrigo's *Concierto de Aranjuez*, but some of the best performances are by Pepe Romero, Narciso Yepes, and John Williams.

Blues

B. B. King's *The Best of B. B. King* (MCA, 1999) is a good introduction to his music, whereas *Lucille and Friends* (Universal, 2003) features B. B. (and the guitar he nicknamed "Lucille") playing alongside other musicians, such as Stevie Wonder and U2.

Muddy Waters, *Hard Again, I'm Ready*, and *King Bee* (all Sony, 2004)

Folk

Paco de Lucía features on several flamenco CDs, including *Siroco* (Polygram, 1990).

Bill Monroe, *The Country Music Hall of Fame* (MCA, 1996). Although Monroe plays mandolin, he always has great bluegrass guitarists in his groups.

Los Pregoneros del Puerto's *Music of Veracruz* (Rounder, 1992) features mariachi music.

Jazz

John McLaughlin, *Extrapolation* (Polygram, 1991), *The Guitar Trio* (Polygram, 1996, with Paco de Lucía and Al di Meola), or *The Inner Mounting Flame* (Sony, 1990, with the Mahavishnu Orchestra)

Joe Pass's *Virtuoso* (Pablo, 2001) is a great **solo jazz** guitar album.

Django Reinhardt's *Swing from Paris* (Past Perfect, 2004) features the master at work in the 1930s.

Rock

Eric Clapton, *Unplugged* (Reprise, 1992)

Jimi Hendrix, *Experience Hendrix: The Best of Jimi Hendrix* (MCA, 1998)

Stevie Ray Vaughan, *The Essential Stevie Ray Vaughan* (Sony, 2002)

The White Stripes, *Elephant* (V2, 2003)

Timeline of Guitar History

1500 B.C.E. Persian tanbur is one of the earliest guitar-like instruments

1400s Vihuela first played in Portugal

1730s Invention of the six-string guitar

1778 Fernando Sor, guitarist and **composer**, is born. He helped make guitar-playing popular.

1830s Antonio de Torres Jurado develops the Torres guitar. Most modern **acoustic guitars** are like this.

1850 Steel strings developed for guitars

1880s Ukulele is developed in Hawaii, based on the instrument played by a Portugese settler

1893 **Classical** guitarist Andrés Segovia born in Spain

1909 Andrés Segovia gives his first public guitar concerts

1915 McKinley Morganfield born in Mississippi. He later changed his name to Muddy Waters.

1919 Jazz guitarist Django Reinhardt born in Belgium

1931 Rickenbacker's Frying Pan made. It is the first commercially successful **electric guitar**.

1933 First solid body electric guitar, the Vivi-Tone Electric Guitar, is built

1935 Audiovox makes the first electric bass guitar

1940 Joaquín Rodrigo composes the *Concierto de Aranjuez*

1942 Jimi Hendrix born in Seattle. He gets his first guitar at age fourteen.

1944 Muddy Waters switches to the electric guitar, and the electric **blues** sound begins

1954 Fender Stratocaster, the most popular style of electric guitar today, first sold

Glossary

accompany play along with

acoustic guitar guitar with hollow body that is not normally electrically amplified

amplifier machine for electrically amplifying sound waves

amplify make louder

blues style of jazz

bridge wooden support holding strings off the fingerboard

chord several pitches played together

classical formal style of music, usually written for orchestral instruments

composer person who writes music

concerto piece of music played by a solo instrument that is accompanied by an orchestra

country and western widespread musical style from the southern United States mixing pop and folk styles

course pair of strings with similar pitch

electric guitar guitar that is always electrically amplified

fingerboard strip of wood on the neck of stringed instruments. The fingers hold the strings against it to change pitch.

folk range of different styles of music from different places, based on traditional, popular tunes

fret raised metal bar on the fingerboard used to play particular pitches

improvise make up music as you play it

jazz style of music with strong, but often irregular rhythm that is part composed and part improvised

nut raised strip at the top of the fingerboard

octave eight notes

orchestra large group of musicians divided into groups of string, brass, woodwind, and percussion instruments

peasant old-fashioned word for a person who works on a richer person's land

pitch musical note caused by sound waves vibrating at a particular speed

pluck pick or pull a taut (tight) string

rock style of loud, popular music featuring electric guitars

solo play without accompaniment

sound hole hole in the center of the guitar that lets sound waves out

sound wave moving pulses of air we hear as sounds

sounding board wooden front of a guitar, used to amplify vibrations from strings

string instrument member of a family of musical instruments played by plucking, strumming, or bowing strings

strum brush across several strings

tuning peg metal peg and cog used to adjust string tension

vibrate move back and forth at a particular speed

Further Resources

Books

Bay, William. *Classic Guitar for the Young Beginner*. Pacific, Mo.: Mel Bay, 2004.

Dick, Arthur. *Absolute Beginner Guitar*. New York: Amscoe, 2002.

Hooper, Caroline. *Learn the Electric Guitar*. Tulsa, Okla.: EDC, 1997.

Kallen, Stuart A. *The Instruments of Music*. San Diego: Lucent, 2003.

Knight, M. J. *Sound Effects*. Mankato, Minn.: Smart Apple Media, 2005.

Turner, Jessica Baron. *SmartStart Guitar: A Fun, Easy Approach to Beginning Guitar for Kids*. Milwaukee: Hal Leonard, 1997.

DVDs

Andres Segovia: In Portrait (BBC/Opus Arte, 2005)

Eric Clapton: Unplugged (Reprise/Wea, 1997)

Websites

http://www.emplive.org/site_map/index.asp
Visit this website of the Experience Music Project to hear what different electric guitars and basses sound like when played by top rock, blues, and jazz musicians.

http://www.playmusic.org

This website lets you create your own musical compositions and helps you find teachers in your area.

http://www.musiceducationmadness.com/guitar.shtml#
Find out how to play different chords using tabs.

http://www.iserv.net/~northwds/Lesson1.htm
Want to play guitar around the campfire? This website will show you how.

Index